JAMES BRANCH CABELL AND THE MODERN TEMPER: THREE ESSAYS

by

RAYMOND HIMELICK
Purdue University

THE JAMES BRANCH CABELL SERIES

REVISIONIST PRESS
New York   1974

© 1974 by Raymond Himelick
This edition is limited to 200 copies.

———

THE REVISIONIST PRESS
G.P.O. Box 2009
Brooklyn, N.Y. 11202

Library of Congress Catalog Card Number: 74-49
ISBN: 0-87700-207-X

Printed and bound in the United States of America

Acknowledgments

To *The South Atlantic Quarterly* for "Cabell, Shelley, and the "Incorrigible Flesh" and "Cabell and The Modern Temper."

To *Modern Fiction Studies* for "Figures of Cabell."

TABLE OF CONTENTS

		Page
I	Cabell, Shelley, and the "Incorrigible Flesh"	1
II	Figures of Cabell	9
III	Cabell and The Modern Temper	16

CABELL, SHELLEY, AND THE "INCORRIGIBLE FLESH" (1948)

WHEN THOMAS JEFFERSON spoke of "the pursuit of happiness" he was thinking of a political right; but sensitive men are forced early into the uncomfortable conviction that happiness, even when made a legal pursuit by constitutional guarantee, still remains coyly elusive. It is probably no accident, therefore, that by the process of pathetic fallacy happiness is given feminine characteristics; and it is significant that to all men at some time or other the personification is identified with a person. Happiness, in short, ceases to be *like* a woman; she *is* a woman; and for a while at least woman is happiness. She is happiness because in the none too impartial eye of man she is the incarnation of love and beauty, of passion and companionship. And it is for these things that all men long—sensitive men most of all.

It is not strange, therefore, that in the work of Shelley, the romantic poet, and Mr. Cabell, the poetic romancer, we find this intense preoccupation with man's hopeful and determined quest for beauty and harmony of existence that is somehow epitomized by the woman dream. With Shelley, the search for the ideal love, carried on in his personal life with rather more vigor than discretion, resulted in the scandalized indignation of a good many people—and in some of his most remarkable poetry, notably "Epipsychidion." Mr. Cabell, content to view the pursuit with quizzical detachment, has produced a series of beautifully written "comedies" which once raised more virtuous eyebrows than the personal gallantries of Shelley. And each artist is ultimately confronted by the insuperable barrier that balks the pursuit—the "incorrigible flesh."

It is a durable and a persistent dream that we cherish, the origin of which Shelley identified as a kind of spiritual loneliness. Every man carries within himself "the chasm of an insufficient void" as well as a "something . . . which thirsts after its likeness." This "something" gives him no rest; it pricks him on unceasingly in the search for this "sister of the soul." Mr. Cabell puts the matter a little more modestly: not its own likeness is the quarry of that restless "something," but a communion with that which is "more fine and potent than itself." Impelled by a dim longing for this "withheld perfection," man wanders into matrimony, perhaps, and with cautious reticence avoids discussion of the subject. Or he may turn artist and give his illusion "secondary employment."

If Shelley's essay "On Love" provides the key to "Alastor" and "Epipsychidion," no less clearly does *Beyond Life* reveal the motive behind the slapdash ardor of Jurgen, Dom Manuel, Florian de Puysange, and Jose Gasparilla. But the miasma of reality smothers all but the most fleeting glimpses of perfection; the chasm still yawns between the fact and the dream. In each case the dilemma is the same. What remedy against the horns?

In "Alastor" there is the strong suggestion of a solution which Shelley himself showed an understandable reluctance to accept in practice. The "veiled maid" who appears in the Poet's vision is indicative of his desire to find the ideal woman embodied in the flesh. She is the "sister of the soul," the likeness of the thirsting "something."

> Knowledge and truth and virtue were her theme,
> And lofty hopes of divine liberty,
> Thoughts the most dear to him . . .

but at this stage the young man is disinclined to accept an assembly of congenial virtues without a becoming corporeal frame. Whatever her theme, she appears in a form not unattractive to the senses, with

> Her glowing limbs beneath the sinuous veil
> Of woven wind, her outspread arms now bare,
> Her dark locks floating in the breath of night,
> Her beamy bending eyes, her parted lips,

and it is significant that his immediate reaction is a normal physical response to such a stimulus. The embrace, however, dispels the dream; and in the subsequent pursuit of this phantom of the ideal, the carnal features show a progressive diminution, as the pursuit of love becomes the pursuit of death, in whose realm we are to understand the woman dream resides. At the end of the quest the Poet has freed himself from the witchery of the flesh, and nothing physical remains of the vision except "two starry eyes, hung in the gloom of thought." Thus the search ends in death and in a mystic union, perhaps, with the ideal. The search for an earthly embodiment of the perfect love is doomed to inevitable failure because of the antithesis of spirit and sense.

A reasonable conclusion, perhaps, for an elderly philosopher; but small comfort to a young poet. Little wonder that in his later work Shelley continued to grapple with this dualism which thwarted the protagonist of "Alastor," to attempt some kind of fusion of the real and the ideal. In "The Sensitive Plant," confronted by the mutability of all lovely shapes and colors and odors, by the disintegration of beauty into obscene shreds of putrefaction, Shelley refuses to admit that the quest for the lovely and lovable is balked by what we are pleased to call reality. The epilogue is an affirmation of faith that it is the external semblance of things that is ultimately tenuous and unreal. We are "the shadows of the dream" and

> For love, and beauty, and delight,
> There is no death nor change. . . .

Like his own Poet, Shelley was divesting his vision of earthly accouterments and moving closer to "reality" of the Platonic Idea. Love was becoming an inseparable component of his Intellectual Beauty and thus, as Solve suggests, "superior to Fate, Time, Occasion, Chance, and Change." It is a wistful conclusion, induced by the "instability of all but weeping," by the general perishability of all earthly symptoms of the "Thou" mentioned in "The Zucca," "whom seen nowhere, I feel everywhere." But a few months earlier he had believed, briefly, that he had found the embodiment of "Thou" in Emilia Viviana. "Epipsychydion," resulting from the temporary enchantment with which Shelley had invested her, is his most impassioned attempt to fuse the ideal and the physical. It is no mere sexual union that he is concerned with: in "Emily" he seeks communion of spirit, the "shadow of that idol of my thought." Resolutely turning his back upon the biological aspects of "dull mortality," he invites her to unite herself with "the imperishable . . . me," but in his anticipation of this excursion into love's more rarefied atmosphere there is a delight so keen that it borders upon, perhaps blends with, physical passion:

> Our breath shall intermix, our bosoms bound,
> And our veins beat together; and our lips,
> With other eloquence than words, eclipse
> The soul that burns between them.

There is a certain droll irony in the fact that even the vestal ecstasy of the spirit can with difficulty be expressed in terms other than those of mundane flesh, and the cynic or the materialist might, without too much obtuseness, construe the lines above as a rather picturesque description of the delights of sin. But Shelley passes quickly from the physical to the metaphysical in an amazing demonstration that succeeded in endowing the anticipated union of souls with something of the rapturous prospects of the bridal chamber:

> The fountains of our deepest life shall be
> Confused in passion's golden purity,
> As mountain-springs under the morning Sun.
> We shall become the same, we shall be one
> Spirit within two frames. . . .

But if in "Epipsychidion" Shelley attains to at least an approximation of the fusion of the real and the ideal, it is to be remembered that this is art. And Mr. Cabell has repeatedly pointed out that only in art are such things possible, for it is the substance of his thesis that in the matter of love, among other things, art is able to accomplish much where life itself ineffectually bungles. Man is "a monarch of dreams incarcerated in a prison of flesh; and . . . hourly fretted . . . by the indifference of nature to his plight," he takes his revenge on the prison by inventing romances in which his lot is immeasurably more splendid, the rewards more in keeping with his really spectacular attainments. Thus the artist may—and should—"prevaricate tenderly about the universe"; it is his duty "stupendously to play the fool" and thus invest this life with a beauty and significance that is not readily apparent in the paraphernalia of reality. So, in the interests of a beauty and significance that ought to be, Mr. Cabell deals cavalierly with things that are merely possible, and his sturdy nympholepts achieve uncommon success here and there as they attempt to realize the woman dream. Jurgen, Dom Manuel, Florian, Perion—each of them has better than average luck with ladies of more than average charm, and some of them are in a fair way to be granted what seems for the moment to be their heart's desire.

It is precisely at this point that Mr. Cabell ceases to be palatable to those whose criterion of romance is, let us say, *Monsieur Beaucaire*. For Jurgen, in spite of his just dealing with a series of beauties as amenable as comely, returns in the end to his wife, for whom he has a very moderate enthusiasm; and he reflects rather wistfully that all of the spectacularly alluring ladies whom he had been permitted to know had been, somehow, not quite satisfying. There was still a part of him, it seemed, that had never quite been touched; furthermore, for all her shrewish garrulity, his wife understood him and was really a superb cook. Besides, he was used to her.

Here is the ironic counterpoint which Mr. Cabell plays against the naïve *ave* to the dream of supernal beauty. The implacable yearning of man serves its purpose, in that through it "the groans of the lover may be perpetuated in the wails of the infant," but it is, after all, a vision of quite remarkable lubricity; and his heroes conclude that it is not the part of sensible men to subject it to any clinical scrutiny. So it is that Jurgen warily declines the favors of Helen, preferring to retain his "unreasonable dreams" and unsatisfied longing rather than run the risk of finding that her beauty was not quite what he had been led to believe. There is the jest of which man is the butt: given the power of superlative dreams, he also possesses the dismal knack of foreseeing the inexorable triumph of the commonplace, the knowledge that to have perfection in his grasp is to find it flecked and marred. Perion discovers that the peerless Faraway Princess has undergone a mysterious metamorphosis into the rather humdrum woman that he married. Florian de Puysange dies disenchanted by possession; Gerald Musgrave returns to the routine comforts of domesticity; and Felix Kennaston sees Ettare, the vision of feminine perfection, vanish like the maid in "Alastor" when he reaches out to her. It is the essence of Domnei that the supreme love and beauty must be "something not quite accessible, something not quite understood." Once the dream is run to earth and foolishly seized upon, it becomes something of the earth. It becomes, in short, a reality; and between the real and the ideal Mr. Cabell finds no kinship. The luckless lover, wooing with ill-advised ardor a golden shadow, wins all the substance and is subsequently pained at the disappearance of the shadow.

Thus, like Shelley, Mr. Cabell confronts the baffling problem of dualism, the antithesis of shadow and substance. Like Shelley, he discerns man's arduous striving for a shadow, "that ageless, lovable and loving woman of whom all poets had been granted fitful, broken glimpses." Like Shelley, he is aware that this dream, which is inexorably interrupted by the reality of substance, is, after all, only a part of man's craving for a beauty and harmony not readily apparent in the world that he knows.

Now from a strong distaste for the disheveled and meaningless slovenliness of reality it is sometimes no long step to the hope-nourished conviction that the shadow may actually be truth dimly prefigured, and the substance only an illusion. In the "Letter to Maria Gisborne" Shelley speaks of

> . . . this familiar life, which seems to be
> But is not . . .

and Felix Kennaston toys with the same notion in *The Cream of the Jest*. But at this point the reactions of the poet and the novelist to the "incorrigible flesh" show interesting dissimilarities. Both are aware that "dull mortality" has an irritating way of substituting itself for the "golden-hued shadow," but oddly enough it is Shelley, the good Platonist, who deplores with more vehemence the transience of earthly forms. In the midst of his passion for beauty as an Absolute, he reveals his dejection over the impermanence of those emotions fostered, and hampered, by the clay. The dream of supernal loveliness appears to be born of a passionate regret for the decay of this world's beauty, and from the dream he "wakes to weep."

On the other hand, there is little of the *ubi sunt* motif in Mr. Cabell's work. The "long, high, fruitless questing" of man is not, after all, concerned with any quite tangible form; and even Guenevere, in the dewy charm of her pre-Launcelot days, was not quite what Jurgen was looking for. Man must be content with the dream alone; for it is the dream, luckily abetted by his own "vanity and hypocrisy and lack of clear thinking," which in the long run proves his salvation. Because of his inordinate capacity for visions, he makes the best of his Dame Lisa as a temporary makeshift, without quite realizing that the Freydis or Helen of his desire is saved from becoming another Lisa by being unattainable. As a "dynamic urge," therefore, the dream is vastly important; but its realization is rendered impossible by what Parrington calls "the curse of possession." In the flesh we live, and because of it we fail in the pursuit of an ideal. It is the mortal substance of the pursuer, no less than that of the pursued, that cheats him. Because of that we all parody that which we see: "We play false to the dream, and it evades us, and we dwindle into responsible citizens." It is decreed that the golden shadow must forever be inaccessible, that Koschei, arbiter of things as they are, must assert the supremacy of the commonplace.

"Fool!" growled Carlyle, "the Ideal is in thyself, the impediment too is in thyself!" With this dictum, Mr. Cabell seems to be in complete agreement. He merely adds, with imperturbable serenity, that the "forked Radish, with a head fantastically carved" is a bit too much of an impediment. Whereas Shelley believed with stubborn faith in the perfectibility of man through the elimination of error and ignorance, Mr. Cabell is convinced that it is only because of man's spectacular muddiness of intellect and his invulnerable thickheadedness that he is permitted to entertain grandiose notions of his destiny. While the ape wallows in his own filth, he gibbers grandiloquently of his kinship with gods and dreams of a beauty wholly inaccessible. It may be that his dream stirs him to emerge from his cell of reality, but he has no real hope of a protracted stay. In the end he must return to the "dull contentment" of what he is used to.

It is clear, then, that behind the mask of the indomitable romanticist there is the leer of a Swift or of a Carlyle. As Professor Beach has pointed out, he has none of the savagery of the former and little of the evangelical earnestness of the latter; but, like them both, he has an abundance of scorn and pity for the race of man. Although he says that to seek possession of love is "to invite inevitable tragedy" and that "the true right tragedy is enacted on the stage of a man's soul, with man's reason as lone auditor," for him—possibly because reason *is* the lone auditor—the tragedy becomes comically grotesque. Romantic passion, easily overwhelmed by romantic appetite, sees the latter annihilated by consummation; every dream of man comes equipped with its own nemesis. Urania, by some inexplicable process, develops a striking resemblance to Pandemos, and pursuit of the shadow ends in perspiring embraces of solid flesh. Mr. Cabell views all this with what Clifton Fadiman calls "pessimism without pain." The case is quite hopeless, but not demonstrably serious.

It is this tendency to observe the quest for love and its attendant failure with equable unconcern for anything more than its risible qualities that is one of the distinguishing marks of the Cabellian attitude as opposed to the Shelleyan. There was nothing tranquil in the poet's striving: it was typical of him that, at his first notion of what he called Intellectual Beauty, he shrieked in ecstasy. Believing with an impervious optimism that ignorance and error alone stand in the way of our attaining the supernal beauty and, therefore, love, Shelley refused to accept as final the verdict of reality. Mourning with dolorous outcries the temporary victories of the substance, he nevertheless remained rapt in his vision of "the white radiance of eternity," confident of the eventual achievement of the ideal, even though in death.

To Mr. Cabell such a vigorous adherence to the dream is, perhaps, a little macabre, and his pessimism is rather more cheerful than Shelley's optimism. Mr. Cabell is an unruffled skeptic with a strong relish for humor, and Shelley was a reformer with, as Matthew Arnold genially put it, "an inhuman want" of it. But humor is only another way of reacting to sorrow and to pity. Shelley, convinced of the heaven of achievement, was not aware of the pathetic comedy of striving; as Mark Twain said, there is no humor in heaven. It is the Cabellian hero who, seeing his brave dreams fail because his own blundering flesh must parody them, has no other recourse but laughter.

FIGURES OF CABELL (1956)

SOME MONTHS AGO James Branch Cabell wrote a probable period to a long, long career with the publication of his memoirs, *As I Remember It: Some Epilogues in Recollection* (McBride). More recently (April 21, 1956) *The New Yorker* gave over something like twenty-five pages to an essay by Edmund Wilson "reopening" the "case" of Cabell. For readers on, say, the unfavorable side of forty the two events, especially when taken in conjunction, may have had some interest.

Cabell's case has, unquestionably, been almost hermetically sealed for roughly a quarter of a century. Although the dust-jacket blurb of the memoirs describes them as "long-awaited," this can be set down as the predictable fantasy of the publisher. So far as I know, the book occasioned little stir beyond the possible nostalgia of some oldsters who, remembering the days when Cabell was very much in fashion, may have murmured, *"Eheu, fugaces!"*

But Wilson has decided that the time for interment is not yet. Coming back to the Virginian's books after twenty years, he takes up a position vigorously at odds with that of most recent criticism, which has either summarily tossed out the baby with the bath water or—more frequently—excitedly denied that the baby was ever there. He does not consider V. L. Parrington's famous eulogy of the twenties, "The Incomparable Mr. Cabell," a brow-raising aberration in taste. He even makes room for a superlative or two of his own: Cabell, he thinks, is a comic poet of "almost unexampled splendor," and Poictesme is notable for its "quicksilver phantasmagoria," which is the author's criticism of life.

Now this, to be sure, is by no means a new note; but it is patently one which has not been blown often or with such authority in the past two decades. The insistent tune in what Cabell criticism has come out during that period has dismissed him as "flossy" and "sophomoric"—a fatiguing exquisite whose concept of existence is simple, monotonous, and monstrous and whose Poictesme is about as appealing to the adult mind as pastoral poetry or Barnabe Googe.

So much, as far as this paper is concerned, for the market quotations. To the critics who manipulate literary stock, God's hinder parts are often no less changeable than accessible. With the appearance of the memoirs and Wilson's essay, however, the time seems appropriate for a review of that estimate of life which, as Cabell's latest work testifies, he has seen no occasion to revise. I prefer to content myself largely with exegesis: simple or no, his philosophy has been both attacked and defended for what it is not. And to no small degree the misapprehension—delightedly abetted by Cabell himself—has been encouraged by the confused alarms stirred up in the camps of Realism and Romance, where a very great deal of clashing goes on in the night of multiple referents.

In *The Counterfeiters* Gide speaks of "the resistance of facts" to the ideal, the rivalry between the real world and the representation of it which we make to ourselves: "The manner in which the world of appearances imposes itself upon us, and the manner in which we try to impose on the outside world our own interpretation—this is the drama of our lives." This has been Cabell's theme in book after book, and he has handled it quite explicitly. For more than a quarter of a century, as a matter of fact, he has been recoiling with elaborate distaste from the "world of appearances" and all the literature which makes that world its subject. Dreiser's work, he thought, was too much like everyday life ever to be suppressed into actual popularity; and the height of all mortal romanticism was "the strange faith of a 'realistic' writer that his wretched book ought either to be written or published." More impersonally, he has consistently argued that the naturalists and realists chase the wrong hare. "No man," as he puts it in *Smire*, "lives in the external truth, among salts and acids, among buying and selling, nor amid any doings outside his own skull . . . for in the warm, phantasmagoric chamber of his brain lives every man vaingloriously, among the painted walls and the storied windows. . . ." And in his autobiography he parallels Huxley's remark that the difference between fiction and life is that fiction makes sense, whereas life usually doesn't: being "true to life" is as patently impossible as it is undesirable, for no one can put into words the complexity of even one moment of human consciousness and every writer of whatever "school" is constrained to edit his world of things, to give it symmetry and incisiveness.

But perhaps this is all too explicit. Assisted by such ostentatiously anti-realistic pronouncements, a great many readers have found in Cabell's fiction a prettified Cloud Cuckoo Land custom-tailored for tastes too dainty for this world. I suspect, however, that this is an inadequate estimate, perversely encouraged by Cabell's linguistic virtuosity.

In *Beyond Life* he gives his voice to an imaginary novelist named Charteris, who develops the Cabellian point of view to its fullest. Ostensibly that view is a defense of romance and the romantic spirit. Humanity, he declares, has always prefigured man as the hero of a cosmic fairy tale, and only this imperturbable confidence in a glorious day after tomorrow has kept man on "the preferable side of Bedlam." Very early in the history of the race it must have become unpleasantly evident that most animals excelled him in strength, that his senses were inferior to those of many insects, that he was deprived of the luxury of wings and even "the common comfort of a tail." What more natural, therefore, than that he solace himself with the rumor that he *did,* after all, surpass the rest of creation in the power of reason; "and, even so, was apparently too magnanimous to avail himself of the privilege."

Naked and powerless and surrounded by other animals "puissant with claw and fang and sinew, an ape reft of his tail, and grown rusty at climbing, was the most formidable, and in the end would triumph." So he consoled himself. And individually and collectively, Charteris continues, men have retained this indomitable faith in the irrational. His material universe is "an endless inconceivable jumble of rotatory blazing gas and frozen spheres and detonating comets," and through this awesome infinity spins Earth, a "blown molecule" crawling with billions of parasites. These parasites beget and dream and kill and toil, just as did all the interminable procession of parasites before them—and each is convinced that his life is a personal transaction between himself and Omnipotence, that what he does is somehow consequential.

Thus Cabell presents his case for the Demiurge, the dynamic illusion, the Ibsenian life-lie which out of our eager vanity creates a world preferable to the one we know, and which assures us—even as we scrabble about in our own filth—that we are a little lower than the angels.

Consider, Charteris goes on, what this demiurge does for love. Just as romance whispers to man of a withheld perfection of symmetry, clarity, and beauty which the devout identify with God, so it convinces him in his youth that woman is a kind of promissory note. He dreams of her as the embodiment of warmth and companionship and a passion that never stales. She is meaning and purpose made flesh, and in pursuit of these things man wanders—as Cabell puts it—into matrimony.

Now it requires no profound suspicion of motives, I think, to detect the duplicity in this championing of romance. We are told that it takes only a talent for the obvious to notice that the "real" world consists for the most part of "ugly and stupid persons doing foolish things" and that if we consider these things too long we may become despondent of the outcome. But romance nourishes optimism: "Thus it is alone that, in defiance of the perturbing spectacle of man's futility and insignificance, as the passing skin trouble of an unimportant planet, he can still foster hope and urbanity and all the other gallant virtues, serenely knowing all the while that if he builds without any firm foundation his feat is but the more creditable."

It is a specious sort of romanticism, certainly, which delights in a judicious blend of paranoia and intellectual astigmatism. One recalls Swift's definition of happiness as "the sublime and refined point of felicity, called, the possession of being well deceived; the serene peaceful state, of being a fool among knaves." Man takes his choice: he can be unhappy or he can be a fool. Cabell's alternatives are no more attractive; if the romantic spirit were any less vital than it is, it could hardly survive such defenders. As Guy Holt once observed, Cabell resembles the Welsh retainers of Edward III, who in battle are said to have crawled about under the horses, impartially knifing friend and foe alike.

This tongue-in-cheek method characterizes his fiction as well. Taking his stance as the dauntless champion of escapism, he insists that literature is a criticism of life only in the sense that prison breaking is a criticism of the penitentiary. The writer's job is to "write perfectly of beautiful happenings," but an examination of some of his escapes is illuminating.

By all odds, of course, the best-known is *Jurgen*. Here a paunchy, middle-aged pawnbroker with a tiresome and shrewish wife is allowed to relive a year of his youth—without losing the knowledge and experience of his forty years. With old head on young body he nonchalantly assumes, one after the other, the titles of duke and prince and emperor and pope. He descends into hell and he ascends into heaven. He swaggers through a series of tireless gallantries with a whole gaggle of charmers—with Dorothy, whom he had loved when he was twenty and a poet; with Guinevere in her dewy pre-Arthur, pre-Launcelot days; with Anaitis, sultry Lady of the Lake; with a plump and domestic wood nymph; with an attractive vampire who deplores the late hours her work entails. He visits the bedchamber of Helen, the paragon of feminine beauty. But at the end of his journey, offered his choice of these more than ordinarily prepossessing creatures, he rejects them all and willingly returns to his pawn shop, his paunch, his wrinkles, and his commonplace wife, for whom he has a very moderate enthusiasm. None of these ladies, he reflects, seemed to have been quite what he had in mind; and Dame Lisa was, after all, a superb cook. Besides, he was used to her.

In *Figures of Earth*, two years after *Jurgen*, Cabell's protagonist is a swineherd whose greatest desire is to mold out of clay and, in the manner of the gods, inspire with life certain figures in his own image. But necessity makes a man of affairs out of the artist: he is obliged to turn aside from his figures to redeem and rule the kingdom of Poictesme and to behave as becomes a successful man and a public figure. He puts aside Suskind, his fairy mistress who personifies the idealism of his youth, and he spends thirty years winning Niafer, who turns out to be much like any other wife. He spends his energies on the duties of ruling, which he finds a crashing bore; but when Suskind tempts him to return, he excuses himself on the grounds that he owes something to his daughter, although privately he finds her a bore too. And eventually he goes to meet Grandfather Death with genuine relief.

So runs the theme. In *Domnei* Perion's Faraway Princess becomes the rather ordinary woman whom he has married. In *The High Place* Florian hacks his way through battalions of monsters and dragons to win the perfect maiden, immured in her enchanted castle with the holy saint Hoprig. Brought down from the high place, however, she dwindles into a stupid and garrulous woman; and Florian is relieved to discover that the child he thought she was bearing him is really the responsibility of the saint. Without the "high place" of enchantment and romance, both beauty and holiness are demonstrably phony.

In *Something About Eve* Gerald Musgrave overcomes sundry obstacles, including the fancier lures of sexuality, in his journey to Antan, the Never-Never land of this novel. Almost within sight of his goal he meets Maya of the Fair Breasts. Maya is plain and not very bright and impatient with all romantic questing; but she cooks well, she darns his socks, she allows him to think he has seduced her and—best of all—she gives him a pair of spectacles which pleasantly enhance the drabness of her person and surroundings. Eventually Gerald never lays aside his spectacles. And he never gets to Antan.

Examples could be multiplied, but the pattern should be clear enough. First man imagines a shining goal where contentment may be found, a high-hearted existence of beauty and meaning and distinction. Then there is the quest for this shining goal, and finally the falling short. Or—sometimes—the attaining of it and the subsequent discovery that it has been lost in the finding.

Reduced to synoptic terms, any literary theme is trite; and this is no exception. One recalls the hankerings of Faust, the cosmic guessing of Ahab and Ishmael, the Gants' frustrated search for "the Father." One also remembers that the jaded author of *Ecclesiastes* long ago observed a certain bromidic quality in life itself; and what Cabell has repeatedly given his readers is a secular and irreverent Everyman, a kind of cynical Morality demonstrating the reiterative staleness of the human spectacle.

His sets and props, of course, employ all the hocus pocus of romance. His pilgrimage drifts through fairy lands where obstacles are never insurmountable and where his heroes are bolstered by charms, talismans, and helpful agreements with more-than-human powers. Here, then, is a "fairer" world than reality, one such as men might create for themselves had they the power of God. But the fairness is illusory: here too men are vitiated by greed, vanity, deceit, and lust. Jurgen's boon of a year of recaptured youth comes to little more than a chance to repeat old errors, with the disadvantage of being able to recognize follies in advance of the commission.

The trouble, as Cabell keeps pointing out, is that man is a two-in-one creature hamstrung by his own dualism, by the antithesis of soul and substance, the ideal and the real. Of the shortcomings of this "incorrigible flesh" he is as acutely conscious as any anchorite itching in his hair shirt. A Donne could contemplate the "subtle knot" of spirit and sense, and comfort himself with the image of body serving as the book to publish soul's mysteries. But for Cabell the book leaves much to be desired. Aside from its impermanence and the predictable imperfections of format, it is always corrupt and inadequate in text. When love's spiritual mysteries, for instance, are reduced to print here, we may have a comfortable, routine affair which serves its purpose in that, as he puts it, "the groans of the lover may be perpetuated in the wails of the infant"; but this pedestrian tale is at best never much more than a pleasant parody of that lyrical wonder we began with.

So man is the butt of a cosmic joke: given superlative dreams and immortal longings, his best efforts ensure the curse of possession and the triumph of the commonplace. Jurgen queries Mother Sereda, a dingy and omni-present female deity, about her job. She replies that she is the goddess of all Wednesdays: she bleaches. The hero of *Cream of the Jest* conjures up with the aid of his magic talisman a vision of feminine perfection who vanishes like mist when he reaches out for her. The moral, we are told, is that the supreme love and beauty must be "something not quite accessible, something not quite understood." The talisman, parenthetically, is the lid of a cold cream jar. And when Jurgen finds himself gazing at the sleeping form of Helen, with her husband conveniently absent, he behaves with a wary circumspectness that has nothing to do with propriety. Rather, he has come to suspect that the thing that keeps Helen from being as routine as his wife is the fact that she isn't his wife. In these somewhat perverse terms Cabell makes a case for monogamy.

A number of years ago critics liked to find Faustian overtones in the Cabellian quest. If there is a parallel, however, the suave Mephistopheles of Goethe furnishes it with his pejorative quip about the vainglorious and abortive flights of grasshopper-man. In Cabell, aspiration modestly lowers its sights: with only mild regret Faust accommodates his "So fair" to second or third best and settles for a plumpening Gretchen and a two-car garage.

For all humanity the grotesque comedy is the same. Romantic passion succumbs to romantic appetite, and romantic appetite is annihilated by consummation. As in Frost's "Nothing Gold Can Stay," Eden sinks to grief with the knowledge of experience. Every dream of man comes equipped with Nemesis built in, and the pursuit of a golden shadow ends absurdly in perspiring embraces of too, too solid flesh.

Nothing in the human spectacle has intrigued Cabell more than this wonderful absurdity. Indeed, he has found little more than that in it. Where some have wept, some have railed, and some have consoled themselves with the hope of ultimate union with God, Cabell—to borrow Ellen Glasglow's words—"refuses to break either his head or his heart." He rejects savage indignation, moral earnestness, Christian faith—and even despair. With unruffled urbanity he dismisses every meaning except the laughable ones and offers his readers, in Clifton Fadiman's phrase, "pessimism without pain." The situation is hopeless, but not serious; and the world ends with neither a bang nor a whimper, but with a well-bred shrug.

This is to say that, though Cabell's juggling act with the two worlds of fact and ideal makes a dexterous show of the one labeled "romance," he is really—as Mencken long ago pointed out—"the most acidulous of all the anti-romantics." He rejects the romantic postulate of the supreme value of the individual, and he scrupulously avoids the romantic predilection for agonizing over supernal injustice. "All our best-thought-of theories about the universe," he remarks in *Straws and Prayerbooks,* "are comparable, let us say, to the knowledge which a fly in a dining-car possesses as to the management of railways." The passage is reminiscent of the observation made by Voltaire's Dervish in *Candide,* but Cabell is never moved to rebel against, or even question, inscrutable evil. Even his most interesting works are marked by this frugality of feeling. "The true right tragedy," he says, "is enacted on the stage of a man's soul, with man's reason as lone auditor." The limiting of the audience is significant and accounts, I suspect, for his dealing with what Leon Howard has called the "literary abstractions of emotion," with "feelings which have been chilled into ideas." Assuming a hostile universe and an ineffectual humanity at odds with the universe and with itself, he equally brushes aside any pretensions to tragedy and insists that his flies take their thought neat —undiluted by sensuous apprehension. The great lesson, he says, is to submit "without either understanding or repining, and without demanding of life too much of beauty or of holiness." One is reminded again of Voltaire's advice to cultivate our gardens, but Cabell's best work is most strongly flavored with his wry delight at man's strenuous effort to gild an abattoir with pastels.

CABELL AND THE MODERN TEMPER (1959)[1]

WHEN LEAR assured Cordelia that in prison they would be as "God's spies," looking into the "mystery of things" and talking of "who's in, who's out," he was not thinking of the vagaries of literary reputation. That area would, however, have been well suited to some kind of supernal scrutiny. One thinks, for example, of Melville—"in" for a time, "out" for a longer time, and now solidly "in" again. And when Edmund Wilson some time ago devoted a lengthy *New Yorker* essay to James Branch Cabell, one was reminded again of this version of the mystery of things.

For a long time, that is, critics and the "passionate" readers Arnold Bennett describes have treated Cabell's work not so much as an art as a syndrome. His penultimate book, *Quiet, Please,* elicited the remark that he was still a "petulant egotist" with a "flossy" style and a sophomoric estimate of life. The Cabell "cult," this notice happily prophesied, would soon enter well-deserved extinction. Throughout the thirties and forties the Virginian's earlier books were given—if anyone deigned to remember them at all—much the same summary dismissal. *Jurgen,* to a reviewer for *The New Republic,* was "a corrupt book, as much in style as in substance, alien and insidious"; the author's philosophy was (*a*) simple, (*b*) monotonous, (*c*) monstrous, and (*d*) "less than half grown-up." In the same diagnostic vein, A. H. Quinn sniffed "an odor of decay about it . . . repulsive to any healthy minded reader," and Granville Hicks

---

[1] This article was written before the death of Mr. Cabell last May. No attempt has been made to revise it with that fact in mind.

brushed aside all of Cabell's work as "a structure of lies . . . mild little fantasies carefully baited with delicate obscenities."

To a good many readers, indeed, both the "obscenities" and the philosophy were bogus. Cabell was merely an exhibitionist who delighted in his own cleverness. The depravity some people found in him was "as synthetic as breakfast cereal, and as harmless." And a few years ago an editor to whom I had sent a paper on the subject returned the manuscript with a stern little note. He himself, he said, could never read the man without retching; and he took a dim view of any criticism which did not clearly share that queasiness.

This has been the general tone of most of the comment on Cabell for the last twenty-five or thirty years, and such severity naturally proceeds from the happy consciousness of critical Election and revealed Truth. Oldsters can recall a time, though, when the tune was very different. To Parrington this was "the incomparable Mr. Cabell," and to an assorted gaggle of other critics he was "the only one of our living literary artists who has worked out something like a truly philosophical concept of human existence," "the possessor of a craftsmanship rarely equaled in American literature," the "master ironist" with "a meticulous perfection of phrasing." He was variously and ecstatically compared with Swift, with Anatole France, with Wilde, with Voltaire, with Sterne. The Cabellian style was a thing of beauty and a joy, if not forever, at least for a decade. Undergraduates—the literate ones—strove to imitate it, and admiring readers ransacked other arts for ways of praising it. Cabell was simultaneously the "Watteau of ironists" and the "Debussy of prose." Even Mencken, not ordinarily addicted to this kind of rhapsody, discovered that the Virginian's language affected him like the music of Brahms.

Now critically speaking, one does not need to be the confidant of a burning bush to suspect that truth sits unobtrusively somewhere between these two magisterial seats of pronouncement. To a degree, of course, the rage for Cabell came for the wrong reasons. Somewhere he remarks that the work of Dreiser was too much like everyday life ever to be suppressed into actual popularity, but unfortunately the banning of *Jurgen* probably did have something to do with Cabell's becoming the center of a cult at least partially composed of the "idiots and prurient fools" he deplores in his recent memoirs. It seems that the book began to sell for as much as forty dollars in the second-hand shops, even after the courts had decided that it was literature, and fit to be read. One suspects, however, that a good many readers went through it with a kind of wild surmise. People who read for erotic stimulation look, as a rule, for more clinical detail than Cabell ever gives; but for a while at least the adaptability of symbol and allegory may have afforded these persons an excitation that seldom found its way to the head.

Still, the zealous devotion of fools has not unduly impeded every man, and it is an oversimplification to attribute Cabell's decline from fashion to nothing more than the fact that his supposed naughtiness grew stale. Of course he has been the victim of changing literary fashions: he never bothered to cultivate social consciousness, for example, or that special kind of earnestness favored when self-conscious damnation began to pall. For that matter, as I am going to try to show, his worlds of Poictesme and Lichfield had little in common, even in his heyday, with the literary conventions and preoccupations of the epoch. It would be just as difficult to account fully for the one-time splendor of his star as for its subsequent fading, I think, but the latter question is the more topical. Actually, of course, it is the same question.

An easy, and not infrequent, answer is the "flossiness" of Cabell's style. What a "corrupt" style is I do not pretend to know, but any reader will concede that Cabell's is involved, ample, tentative—sometimes finical. It is elaborate, devious, Latinate. It purrs along with mannered and preening elegance, whereas we prefer the plain Anglo-Saxon, the honest muscularity of the vernacular. Or so we say. And having said, we accept without notable flinching the convoluted parentheses of Henry James, the Elizabethan rhetoric of Melville, the pronoun wilderness of Faulkner, even the sludgy pedestrianism of Dreiser.

For that matter, style may be the man, but it is always the man dressed and combed for public appearance. Even if he elects to show himself in unbuttoned chambray with hair carefully tousled, he is no less self-conscious. What fourteen-year-old ever talked like Huck Finn? The truth seems to be that, judging from the catholicity of our acceptance, we care less about style than we like to think. Other things, however, may have mattered more.

For one thing, Cabell's current low estate may be the consequence —at least in part—of his systematic quarantine of anything resembling literal reality. I am not speaking of his "romanticism"; he is a good deal less of the romantic than, say, Wolfe or Faulkner or Hemingway. Wilson is right, to be sure, in reminding us that glorifying a "waking dream" is merely to say that one prefers one kind of fictional convention to another. The point is that the dream convention deprives the reader of much that he has a feeling, if ambivalent, regard for. It scrupulously by-passes what Doctor Johnson called "the general heap" of the human condition, the "insect vexations," the trivial impertinences which constitute the "main of life." Not unlike the Existentialists, Johnson saw us as spending our lives burrowing in a thicket of facts. We constantly find ourselves, in Albert Cook's phase, "staring the probable in the face." Existence is a pattern of food to be bought and eaten, teeth to be brushed, fuel bills to be paid, baby sitters to be found, promotions to be hoped for, vitamins to be taken, PTA meetings to attend. However routine and pointless we find the "probables," and whatever nostalgia we imagine that we have for unity and ultimates, these commonplaces attach us to life. No less than Johnson, most of us operate by a rough-and-ready layman's positivism. The world is indeed very much with us, and we seldom convince ourselves that it isn't all we have.

What I am suggesting is that the deliquescent imagery of swords, candles, veils, sigils, and thaumaturgy employed by Cabell is unlikely to be convincing to readers conditioned to thinking of experience in terms of a plethora of literal matter. The "incorrigible flesh," which Cabell has long recognized as the impediment to the dream, may very well be no less an impediment to the acceptance of his fictional convention. It looks in vain for any homely reminder of its factual situation. I suspect that, for a public long accustomed to a diet of even brutally concrete sensory data, the surrogates of Cabell's fictive world have much the same appeal that intravenous feeding would have to a man in the habit of eating at truck stops.

One recalls E. M. Forster's complaint that Henry James seemed reluctant to do a novel until most of human life had disappeared, that his characters were incapable of fun, carnality, or rapid motion. So it is with the inhabitants of Poictesme, Lichfield, and Fairhaven: unless one endows them with the routine substance of "probables," even their philandering has about as much immediacy as, say, a whimsical pen-and-ink sketch of cross-pollination. Now, admittedly Cabell intends them to be this way. It is a deliberate avoidance of life, at least in its more sweaty manifestations. The trouble is, apparently, that we find it increasingly hard to imagine any literature as human in its depths unless it comes equipped with all the familiar appliances. As Lionel Trilling has suggested in *The Opposing Self* (he was discussing Howells, not Cabell), mind and will need a resisting object in the form of "stupid, recalcitrant literal matter."

"What a piece of work is man!" cried Hamlet, and went on to call him "the paragon of animals" and the "quintessence of dust." Alive as any Renaissance humanist to the ironic antitheses involved, Cabell constructs his own paradox by parading the "quintessence," which he sees as deluding man, and exorcising out of existence all reminders of the dust from which it is born. Unfortunately, no matter how much we think we approve of unconditioned spirit, we have trouble extracting it from context. Even a Shelley, one recalls, had to solidify the rarefaction of spiritual union in terms not wholly unsuggestive of the bridal chamber:

> Our breath shall intermix, our bosoms bound,
> And our veins beat together; and our lips,
> With other eloquence than words, eclipse
> The soul that burns between them.

Today, of course, we are uneasily amused at talk about sisters of the soul; but we do have a vast respect for the narcissistic fingering of sensibility, the interior elevator conducting tours all the way down to the subbasement. This is our own vision of inwardness, but it principally reflects our preoccupation with the piecemeal awareness of piecemeal realities. In *Contexts of Criticism,* Harry Levin has noted two strongly marked tendencies in the art of the recent epoch: a lavish concern for the minutiae of existence" and a continuing search for "the primordial, the irreducible, the typical." It is scarcely necessary to remind ourselves that the second tendency could have been born only from the first.

"The true right tragedy," according to Cabell, "is enacted on the stage of a man's soul, with man's reason as lone auditor." His phrasing suggests a significant alienation from the quasi-professional neuroticism which we assume to be the hallmark of modern man. *Soul,* for one thing, is not a currently fashionable word; today's earnest reader has been sicklied o'er with the pale cast of Psychology

101—and rouged somewhat irregularly with selected leaves from Freud, Jung, and Sir James Frazer. The transcendental has been equipped with a new ontology and a new set of words; taking a page from the *Ion* we assume that a writer says more than he knows, but we expect him not to loaf and invite his soul so much as to work and invite the collective-unconscious. Hamlet has long been endowed with an Oedipal delay, Macbeth slashes at the father-image in Duncan, Tristram Shandy's unhappy encounter with the window sash anticipates the anthropological theory of circumcision as a ritualistic substitute for castration, and the Earth-Mother is all but ubiquitous.

I think it likely that Cabell's very considerable erudition does include acquaintance with *The Golden Bough*, but he is apparently no more taken by the continuing search for the archetypal than by the minutiae of existence. When he uses myth—as, say, in *Figures of Earth*—it is part of his satirical machinery, something he elects to employ, not be employed by. And, to return to his remark about reason as the audience of tragedy, one recalls two much admired phrases of Eliot, one concerning the "sensuous apprehension of thought" and the other his praise of the mind of James as "too fine for thought to violate." In much of the widely respected literature of the past half decade, it seems, thought itself has been less important than the way it made people feel when they had it.

These preoccupations Cabell has shrugged off. Nor has he ever catered to what some critics have diagnosed as a taste for grandiose evil. Trilling, for example, finds in us a complicated relation to "the common, the immediate, the familiar, and the vulgar elements in life"; we expect to find these elements in our literature, but we want them "in their extremity" as a kind of "outer limit of the possibility of our daily lives." Thus raised to the nth power, commonplaceness poses a threat. Transcending ordinary lower-case vexation, it is apotheosized into Evil; and Trilling suggests that awareness of evil in this lordly sense confers upon us a kind of spiritual prestige, "a sign that the person has a direct connection with godhead." Whether it is allied with murky sexual cravings, inscrutable nature, or the attritive pressures of the market place, it has a charm of its own. We want it in our literature because disintegration seems more "real" than anything else.

So Wolfe takes arms against—or tries to swallow—a sea of nullities, Faulkner enhances not-unheard-of depravity and decay with a kind of exotic phosphorescence, Melville universalizes a sailing mishap into a myth of primal blackness, and Conrad insists upon a heart of darkness so complete that, as F. R. Leavis has pointed out, we never know just what it is—only that it is "unspeakable," "profound," "inconceivable." And it does make a difference when, as in the Hollywood version, *Moby Dick* becomes the story of a man inordinately vexed with a whale; or when one supplies referents for the "horror" of Kurtz. Even the darkest gods lose something when translated into the context of a morals charge; left sufficiently mysterious they are barely distinguishable from glory.

But Cabell concedes no spiritual prestige to—the phrase is from *Beyond Life*—"the passing skin trouble of an unimportant planet." On the contrary, he dismisses as a part of the saving delusion which keeps us "on the preferable side of Bedlam" this prideful insistence upon a cosmic and anthropocentric malignity. In *Straws and Prayer Books* he compares humanity to dining-car flies presuming to understand—or at least to deplore—the management of railroads. Hell is only the measure of the extravagant emphasis we place upon our moral status, and Jurgen's inferno is filled with importunate spirits insisting that their misconduct be dignified by torments appropriate to Evil.

A romantic has been defined as someone who does not believe in the fall of man, and realism has been described as romanticism on all fours. Obviously, neither the views of human experience suggested by these definitions, nor our relations to these views, are by any means antithetical. We can judge "all fours" only by some intransigent notion of the perpendicular, and to mourn human debasement is to infer a state less unkempt. Gloucester, one recalls, also sees men as flies, flies at the mercy of gods who are like wanton boys; but the image in *King Lear* is less repugnant than Cabell's, I suppose, because it is premised upon the tragic importance of the "flies" and it presupposes supernatural powers with no more pressing engagement than to sport with human lives. It is not too fanciful to say that only *hybris* puts on the sackcloth of despair. Even the most cloacal naturalism can afford us the paradoxical comfort of this concept of centripetal evil. We are tempted to smile, perhaps, at a romantic Omar, darkly muttering into his forbidden wine over the memories of "that Insolence"; but he is not worlds away from Kafka's K. who, as the knife twists in his heart at the end of *The Trial*, cries, "Like a dog!"

In Cabell, however, a self-conscious anguish over the human predicament has been conspicuously absent. If he does not believe in either the fall of man or the "all fours" convention, it is only because, rather like Gulliver's Houyhnhnm, he sees a Yahoo affecting to teeter on its hinder legs. He has much of the imperturbable cheerfulness of Montaigne, for whom, in his memoirs, he owns to a lingering fondness. It may be, as Wilson says, that his urbanity is "a poise never far from a precipice." Still, it never slips over the edge. If we feel impelled to gasp at our vision of the nullity of human experience, it is only because we have been making too elaborate claims for it. Taken on its own terms life is still an interesting—if inconsequential—performance.

Interesting, that is, to the comic spirit, which does not boggle at the possibility that a man's cat may very well think she is playing with him. And interesting not in spite of its inconsequence, but because of it. Mark Twain supposed that there would be no laughter in heaven; nor, presumably, will there be in a hell negatively endowed with the same anthropocentric feeling. In Cabellian comedy, however, the nugatoriness of life is the major premise upon which men erect indomitable *non sequiturs* of dream. Hamlet thinks it strange to reflect that the dust of Alexander is somewhere stopping a bunghole. Cabell's own reflections upon the anticlimactic flesh seldom take the turn of *ubi sunt* homilies, but in his most characteristic work he has been absorbed by the automatism with which this flesh caricatures the dream it creates, the discrepancy between the promise and the performance, the imagining and the obstinate fact. For him the human spectacle is, in small, Bach assaulted with a tin whistle.

And one does not become involved in spectacle, a fact which probably explains that frugality of feeling which many of Cabell's readers have complained of—the refusal, in Ellen Glasgow's words, to break either his head or his heart. An age valuing passionate commitments is likely to consider this relation to his ideas even more suspect than the ideas themselves, but passionate commitments are not for comedy. As Bergson has it, indeed, laughter is always accompanied by the absence of feeling; it has no greater foe than emotion. Shunning the emotive dangers of "things," of literal reality, Cabell's most interesting work has been a parable, an abstract of life's reiterative triviality enlivened by the human gift for rococo self-delusion. The central character is folly itself, and his Florians, Geralds, Manuels, and Perions dance predictable steps to the tune it plays. They represent a composite Everyman, but an Everyman who is largely invisible to himself and all the more absurd for his myopic vision.

So the world goes, in this parable; and its end is hardly consonant with either a bang or a whimper. Clifton Fadiman long ago called this position "pessimism without pain." It is also, of course, a pessimism that is academic, even doctrinaire. It was already venerable when Lucian wrote his *Dialogues* and has had professors at least as recent as Housman—who is no longer very fashionable either. Given those preoccupations I have attempted to outline, we seem unlikely to embrace a cosmic iconoclasm that affronts us with gaiety and a shrug. Carlyle, one recalls, growled at Voltaire for being nothing but a mocker who had never uttered a "great thought," and it is perhaps significant that a recent stage version of *Candide*, according to at least one reviewer, did its best to extinguish the lighted fuse of Voltaire's tale and invest it with sunbursts of radiant affirmation.

For whatever reason, however, the stage *Candide* failed. If this fact is a sign and a portent that mockery may, so to speak, keep its hat on, that negation need not always wear a hair shirt, then the case of Cabell may not be entirely closed.